Poems for Taylor Swift

&

Other Unicorns

by

Various Artists

First published 2025 by The Hedgehog Poetry Press

Published in the UK by
The Hedgehog Poetry Press
Coppack House, 5
Churchill Avenue
Clevedon
BS21 6QW

www.hedgehogpress.co.uk

9 8 7 6 5 4 3 2 1

A CIP Catalogue record for this book is available from the British Library.

ISBN: 978-1-916830-55-4

Contents

PATRICIA M OSBORNE

I think I love you

blares from my transistor radio,
shoots up the Singles Chart.

Baby-faced popstar wins my heart
as the twenty-year-old grasps stardom
in the US musical sitcom on TV.

Could it be Forever circles
my record turntable,

steals number two in the Top Ten.

A bevy of teens wave banners,
scream out his name, raise
autograph books high
but it's mine that he takes.

My heart gallops as his hand
brushes my fingers.

I think I love you I whisper
as he scratches David Cassidy
on the first blank page.

PHIL SANTUS

John, Paul, George and Ringo

John said that writing is easy.
You decide what you want to say,
you make it rhyme and choose the chords.

Easier said than done, I feel,
whilst I'm struggling with my poems,
including these, non-rhyming, words.

Paul said that Eleanor Rigby
was a name that he created
from various random sources,

but, in a Liverpool graveyard,
I've seen poor Eleanor's gravestone -
a strange coincidence or what?

George was a kid in Hamburg days
and learned a thing or two or three,
but he loved his guitar the most.

George hoped that we all are learning -
of this I'm not so sure, myself -
in some ways yes, in others no.

Ringo owns a signature phrase:
'Peace and Love, everybody',
and we should all have more of that.

GRETA ROSS

Yesterday

It had to be him
that babyface for me
the dream of a maybe

oh please please me
but I should've guessed
I'm no sexy princess

too plain for a Beatles' eye
nor for that boy's in class
Paul's lookalike

who never looked at me
but now I get it was all
just transference

the rampage of hormones
longing for *love me do*
long into the night

CELIA JENKINS

LARP (Live Action Role Play)

How did you decide that the best way to discover who you were
Was by being someone else?
Once a month, on a Friday night,
Rushing home from school (after Games, 2:30 – 3:30)
Quick shower, then
Lacing yourself into a corset
A cape
Sticking on elfin ears
Masking your face, curling your hair
While other girls got ready for pub and club
You were heading to the tavern, cavorting
With dwarves and sorcerers,
Healers and archers.

What was this mania
That your school friends couldn't grasp?
The desperation to live half in one world,
Half in another,
To spend weekends bashing grown men
With rubber swords and pole arms
Adventuring in real time,
Not a board game, fate turning
On the twist of a dice,
But in your own hands,
Smeared with mud,
Blackberry thorns ripping a velvet dress,
The rain, really thundering.

Who was that girl, that half-formed woman,
Who decades ago knew herself better
When she used another name
- Aurora, Peasant -
And who is she now,
Sometimes catching echoes on the wind
Of a voice calling out
From another world
Waiting for adventure
To begin?

OLIVIA TODD

Escaping Devolution

Hey, Liv,
your world was already starting
to dismantle,
like jamming the B button
on your silver, Gameboy Advance system
to prevent a favourite Pokémon from evolving.
Much harsher than giving them an Everstone—
but fuck change.
Change equalled a step closer to saying,
'See you never.'
Change equalled accepting he was going
to die sooner
or later,
and there was no save button to pause
progression.
A six-year-old shouldn't be dealing with
this kind of life shit.
But it's okay.
In this pixelated world,
everything's whole.
You're the heroine.
You can't save him, but you can befriend them—
filling up your Pokédex is healthier
than obsessing over
the electrifying calls of a patient yelling,
'Nurse! Nurse! Nurse!'
The disgruntled, shadow-faced health worker
is right next to the elderly lady
whose rocking in a plaid armchair.
Unseen, unheard.
The pale lady knocks over a cup,
and is scalded by tea.
Charizard's flames would've been cooler.

The patient engages in combat by
continuously batting away the nurse's hand,
preventing her from placing a soothing
compress on her burnt thigh.
The old lady is aiming for a KO.
I recoil at the nurse's Quick Claw reprimand,
'It's your fault for spilling it on yourself!'
Like it's my fault I was born
and that's why he got Dementia—
the illogical thought emerges
and vanishes as rapidly as an
Abra.
As we wait for my dad to return from
his ceaseless walking route,
another patient frantically shrieks,
'The ship's sinking! The ship's sinking!'
By comparison, the pixel waters
are serene, minus encountering wild
Pokémon every five sodding seconds.
But it's always a pleasure
discovering a new friend.
Always a pleasure existing
a virtual life that has no end.
As I switch off Emerald, I think,
how peaceful it must be
inside a Pokéball, curled up and dead
to the chaos of St James'.

RACHEL BURROWS

Roots

My best friend loved Shakin' Stevens.
She had posters to prove it.
Her bedroom door was painted green,
she even had a denim jacket.
We were eleven.
I had a sensible coat for *all occasions*
and Hedgerow Flowers on my wall.
I knew their names like she knew lyrics,
and I knew the springtime
of primary was over.
Seeds of teen had been planted.
The lipstick kisses on Shaky's cheek
were as alien to me
as my honeysuckle
was familiar.
We grew apart.
I discovered Madness and Marley,
Armatrading and Cohen.
Became entwined.
Gathered strength.
Reached the sun.
And bloomed at last.

WENDY GOULSTONE

Curtain Call

How did it start?
Ah, yes, a dark auditorium
leaning forward on her mother's lap
peering down over a mass of heads
to that brightly lit stage
where they danced as they sang
Tea for two and two for tea.
She's hooked.

A cardboard cut out model theatre
pipe-cleaner actors
a headful of fairy stories
and before long she's writing plays.
Where next? Of course, Mr Blake
may his name be praised.
Mr Blake who gave her free rein
gave her Story Time - that half hour
before the home bell rang.

And she's off. Am-Dram here she comes.
Homework dashed off in spider script.
See *me about your writing* at the bottom
of every essay. But she doesn't care.
She has lines to learn, rehearsals,
and soon she's reading Shakespeare
Bernard Shaw, Eliot, Anouilh, Bennett, Hare.

She can't stop. Not now. Not ever.
Head spinning plots, characters
dripping off the ends of her fingers
and there's a real live theatre
half a mile away.
Bliss.

GERALD KILLINGWORTH

The Boy Who Wouldn't Say Bum

I can see him now:
alphabetised in the gym
with the other newbies, surnames A to M,
a nervous morning face
but, thankfully, no tears,
pens and pencils safe in the case his younger sister gave him
'For your first day.'
He hasn't had time yet to scratch off the good luck puppy.

They have already removed his first name
and his confidence.
But what language do they speak here
where everything is foreign,
crowded, bound by rules he can't anticipate?
His village-school chatter
won't pass muster with the big boys and girls.
He wishes Stephen wasn't an N to Z.
He'd know the right words for 'I want a wee.'
And if they ask what book he's reading
he's going to say it's about astronauts,
not *Narnia* (for the third time).

He'll have to choose every word carefully from now on,
take his cues from what he hears the Second Form say –
the dread of being laughed at,
being thought a baby.
For reasons that won't go away,
he's terrified of blurting out that one word - *Bum.*
He might need to say it at any time –
'Long trousers chafe my...'
'I fell on my...'
'Shift yer...'
His dad says *arse* to his mates
and Auntie Renee talks *sotto voce* about her *sit-upon.*
He can't risk experimenting with these.
'What did you learn at school today?'
'I concentrated on not saying...'

I want to shout out to him:
Don't wait forty years to copy Clark Gable's
'Frankly, my dear, I don't *give* a damn.'
Don't give a tinker's toss now, or tuppence, or a flying f...
Bum, bum, bum as much as you like.
Life's a bum deal, so kick its bum
and be yourself to kingdom come.
Tarara - *bum* - de - ay
I threw self-doubt away!

LIZ KENDALL

Supermodel Sebastian Bach

Naomi would kill for his leather-clad legs.
Cindy's pouting lips are nothing to his.
Clear wide eyes, faux-shy Lady Di with a hard-on
and hair! bouffant blonde,
shining over shoulders honey-gold, strong.

The legs on him go up and up
the length of him goes up and up
his hair it cascades down and down oh, Rapunzel!
voice swelling surround-sound
expanding into resonant fullness, water-pure vibrato,
wrestling into dirt-earth bear-gruff growl
and every note and possibility in between.

Mic-screaming excess-drinking cock-grabbing
frontman-selfish devil and Jesus waiting in the wings
with his wings; that spare pair so useful for conversion
is always the most glamorous and effective way
to snare new followers. Make them believe.
Conviction is the linking bridge between the devil's music
and the other kind; is all that makes the other kind bearable.

Rock music then had many men more beautiful
than the most beautiful women in the world,
and all while barely eating living on junk food
and pussy nectar and Jack Daniels, vodka;
having the life sucked out of them nightly;
how many beggar-cheap burgers must a young man eat
to produce that lovin' spoonful? Bleak.

But anyway more beautiful he was
than all those supermodels put together, you know the ones:
who wouldn't un-glue one taut eyelid for less than twenty grand
or touch one polished toe to the floor before confirming how much
and that of course, darling, you can keep the clothes.
Smuggle Sebastian into those lineups
he would pass and surpass them all in feminine perfection:
those lips, eyes, sweeping hair, glowing skin,
cheekbones, Christ! the nerve of them to be so fucking fine.
He'd rip that catwalk strut, leave it burning in his wake.

How old were we - my friend and I - perhaps fourteen?
one music magazine ran a several-page spread:
Skid Row and mainly Sebastian; and the realisation
that it would have to be bought in duplicate, or was it triplicate?
Impossible to choose one side and not the other,
so much beauty: more than my pocket money's worth.
Appeals were made and more pages were bestowed.
The bedroom wall could open and receive
onto its remaining pastel-blank virginity
not one but two Sebastians; not three but four: territorial.
Teenage girls are territorial, possessive,
desiring fiercely and it never really wears off.
Beauty - beauty as Oscar Wilde declared,
staked his life on - beauty is a necessity.

A C CLARKE

When Lester Piggott runs the riding-school

after Deborah Finding When David Bowie is my dad

He tells us small is strong, the power is in your thighs
knees are for steering, keep them close to your horse's sides.

He's chest-high to a sixteen-hander. Does that faze him?
Not on your nellie. Once up he's a centaur, blazing

a winning run after holding back to the last minute.
He says *judgement is all* and we'd best start learning it.

We never see him smile even if we're doing well.
It's not his thing. But he doesn't shout when we fail.

Your head and your heart keep up his mantra. We try.
If we take a tumble – we do – his motto is *never say die*

LAURA COONEY

The Need To Believe

It is with terror,
I see that I have dyed,
my forehead orange.

Such was the desire to break,
free from this monotony,
that I,

the sensible one,
went to superdrug on my break
and later in Carol's Bathroom--
did a crazy thing.

In all the years I've watched,
I think I've only seen Scully drink twice.
What would she make of this?

In the end we agree,
the colour isn't actually that bad.

But we can't deny it,
laughing,
It's my forehead,
that shows my shame.

I put the fairy liquid down,
And pick up the Budvar.

I'm still sceptical,
but if I turn my head this way,
or that,
I'm definitely out of this world.

MIRIAM MOORE

For Neil, Who Will Never Read This

Back in the eighties at my all girls' convent school
It was the Alpha males that ruled - Duran and Spandau and Wham
The alternative girls listened to The Smiths and didn't smile much.
Life was tough when you couldn't find your tribe
Or indeed your vibe
And you didn't know what a zeitgeist was, let alone try and spell it

But you were different. An air of detachment
Lyrics just on the right side of pretentious
And music I could move to. At last, I too
Could spend hours in HMV idly flicking through vinyl
And buying German imports. Casually cool
Just like your mate, Chris.
I stuck your pictures on my bedroom wall
And stuck your albums on my turntable
I poured meticulously over your lyrics and wrote fan mail. I shared secrets.

I loved you.

Before I knew what homophobia was people said unpleasant things.
I just laughed it off. Even if all the while I knew I was slightly in denial.
I even earned myself a label. They called me the Pet Shop Girl
They still do. Last year you topped my Spotify unwrapped
And I took my 16-year-old to see you live and as she sang along, I smiled
Well done me. I picked wisely. You've survived.

And yes. I still would.

ALISON BROWN

Well Fancy That!

I wonder what that word is. Love perhaps?
The courtly sense of distance and of need.
A dream-like fancy-dizziness which traps
You in its visceral, hungry screaming greed.
Cassette tapes play and play until they jam;
With posters carefully plucked from centrefolds;
Dark eyes with moody glare: my modern man.
Singing of trips aboard as worlds unfold.
I'd been Waiting for this rhythm to emerge,
Though dimly conscious of its Ghostly tune;
It spoke of finding pleasure in the dirge
of ordinary days and nights that pass too soon.
When Terry sang of having all the fun
I sensed deep in my soul I'd found the one.

PATRICIA M OSBORNE

Bolanmania

Posters shoot up on bedroom walls
speakers blast from record players
vinyl discs spin

Ride a White Swan
rocks the world

Glitter gel teardrops
bejewell Marc's cheeks
his corkscrew locks shimmer
vibrant silk outfits dazzle
as he sashays on stage

Young women scream
hearts bang
pulses pound
as T-Rex boogies

Hot Love   *Telegram Sam*
   Metal Guru
bomb the Top Ten charts

until one September morn

no more rides on a white swan